Our Community Is in a Valley

Lamar Coldwell

Rosen REAL READERS

Rosen Classroom™
New York

This is our community. It is in a valley.

A valley is a low area of land. It is between large hills or mountains.

There are mountains around us.

A river flows down the mountains. It cuts through the valley.

The river empties into a lake in the valley. We fish in the lake.

There are farms in the valley.
Flat land is good for farming.

Words to Know

farms

mountains

valley